My FIRST Book of Prayers

Claire Freedman

Illustrations by Alison Atkins

CANDLE
BOOKS

Hooray for God!

Dear God,
I like praising You.
I like singing to You
   at the top of my voice!
Thank You for everything!
Amen.

Hooray!
You made the giraffe
 as tall as a tree.
Thank You, God.
Hooray! You made the
 caterpillar, ant and bee.
Thank You, God.
Hooray! You made our world,
 so perfectly.
Thank You, God.
Amen.

3

My Family

Dear Lord Jesus,
Thank You for cuddles with
  Mommy and Daddy.
Thank You for hugs
  and kisses.
Dear Lord, thank You
  for giving me so much love.
Amen.

Dear Lord Jesus,
I love my mommy and daddy.
I love my brother and sister.
I love my grandma and
  grandpa.
Please look after them.
Please don't forget to look
  after me too, Lord.
Amen.

Dear Lord,
Thank You for my family.
Thank You for all the people
  who look after me.
Please look after children
  who don't have families
  of their own.
Thank You, God.
Amen.

Dear God,
My uncle and aunt came today.
They brought me a great
  present.
My uncle told us funny jokes.
Thank You for uncles
  and aunts.
Amen.

Dear Lord,
Great news!
My brand new baby sister
  is here at last.
She looks very small, God.
Her fingers are tiny.
I can't wait to play with her.
Please help her grow up
  really fast, so I can.
Amen.

Dear Heavenly Father,
Daddy has to work so hard.
We hardly ever see him.
Please help Daddy at work,
  so he can come home earlier.
Then I can kiss him goodnight
  before I go to sleep.
Thank You,
Amen.

Dear Father in Heaven,
My Daddy has to go away.
Please look after him while he's away.
Please help his work to go well.
And please bring Daddy home
  safe to Mommy and me.
Thank You,
Amen.

Dear Lord,
Sometimes my brother
  makes me mad.
I get fed up with him.
Please help me love my brother
  and get on better with him.
Thank You, Lord.
Amen.

My Friends

Heavenly Father,
My friend broke my toy today.
I know he didn't mean to,
  but it was my special toy.
Please help me to forgive my
  friend.
Amen.

Dear Lord,
Thank You for friends to
  play with.
Thank You that we can
  play games and
  have fun together.
Amen.

Dear Lord,
My best friend has moved.
She lives so far away
 from me now.
I really miss her.
Please help us both to make
 new best friends very soon.
Then we won't feel so sad.
Thank You, Lord.
Amen.

Lord,
Please forgive me.
Today I was unkind
  to my friend.
Please help her to forgive me
  when I tell her I'm sorry.
Amen.

Special Days

Dear Lord,
I had the best birthday party ever.
All my friends came.
They gave me lots of cards and presents.
We played pin-the-tail-on-the-donkey
  and hot potato.
I blew out all the candles on my cake
  in one blow.
Thank You for a
  wonderful
  birthday.
Amen.

School

Dear Lord,
I am starting my new school
   tomorrow.
I am really scared, Lord.
There are big butterflies in my
   tummy.
Please come to school with me,
   and help me make new friends.
Thank You,
Amen.

Heavenly Father,
Thank You for our school.
Our teacher is really kind
    and helpful.
She is good at explaining
    things to me.
Thank You for my teacher
    and my school, Lord.
Our lessons are a lot of fun.
I really enjoy learning things.
Amen.

Dear Lord,
Please help me with my school work.
Sometimes I find it hard.
Please help me to listen to
    my teacher more carefully.
Please help me not to give
    up too quickly when my work
    is difficult.
Thank You, God.
Amen.

Heavenly Father,
Sometimes I'm scared of people at school.
I'm scared of standing up in class.
I don't like it when everyone looks at me.
I'm worried I'll say something wrong and
    everyone will laugh at me, God.
Please help me in school, Lord.
Thank You.
Amen.

Vacations

Dear Lord,
We're off on our vacation
   tomorrow.
I'm so excited.
Thank you for vacations!
Amen.

Dear Lord,
I'm glad that, when we are far
  from home,
  You are still with us.
Please keep us safe.
Amen.

Heavenly Father,
Thank You for all the fun of the seaside.
Thank You for sandcastles
  and sandy beaches.
Thank You for splashing in the waves
  and wading in the sea.
Thank You for shells and seaweed,
  and rockpools to explore.
Thank You for picnics
  and ice creams on the beach.
Thank You for vacations, God.
Amen.

Dear God,
Today we fed the ducks.
Mom saved up all the bread.
They waddled out to say
  "hello",
  all waiting to be fed.

We counted lots of ducklings,
  and heard them say,
  "quack, quack".
Thank You for all the ducks,
  Lord.
I hope we can go back.
Amen.

Sorry

Dear Lord,
I'm sorry I was so naughty
  today.
Please forgive me.
Sometimes I find it hard to
  be good.
Please help me to be
  nicer tomorrow.
Amen.

Dear Heavenly Father,
Sometimes I get all cross inside,
  and have a bad mood day.
I scream and shout and stomp my feet,
  if I don't get my way.

I'm sorry for my bad mood, Lord,
  and I just wanted to say:
  I'm glad that whether I'm good or bad,
  You love me anyway.
Amen.

Dear Lord,
Today I told a lie.
I know it was wrong.
I haven't felt right inside
   ever since.

I'm sorry, Lord.
Please help me
   not to do it again.
Thank you, Jesus.
I feel better now.
Amen.

Dear Lord,
Thank You that when we are
  sorry,
  we can ask You to forgive us.
Thank You that You will
  always forgive.
Amen.

Help Me, Lord!

Dear God,
I am SO disappointed!
I wanted to be picked for our
  school play,
  but I'm going to be a helper.
My friend is in the play.
Please help me to be happy
  for her.
Please help me to be the best
  helper ever.
Amen.

Dear God,
Please help me to stop
   wanting things I know
   Mommy can't afford,
   like expensive dolls and toys.
Please help me to be grateful for
   all the things
   I have already.
Thank You.
Amen.

Dear God

Dear God,
I'm glad You love me.
I'm glad You're looking
  after me.
I feel a lot safer knowing
  that, Lord.
Thank You for everything.
Amen.

Dear God,
Thank You that,
  with You,
  I am never alone.
Amen.

Dear God,
You know all about me.
You know the color of
  my eyes.
You know what I like to
  eat most.
You know when I am happy
  or sad.
And You know what is best
  for me.
Thank You, Lord.
Amen.

Dear God,
Sometimes I don't talk to You –
  but I know You're still there.
Thank You.
Amen.

Prayer Time

Dear Lord Jesus,
Thank You for prayer time.
Thank You that we can talk
  to You about anything.
Anytime.
Anywhere.
Amen.

Dear God,
Thank You that we can tell
  You our secrets:
    things that make us happy;
    things that we worry about;
    things we look forward to;
    things we are scared of.
We can share them all
  with You.
Thank You, Lord.
Amen.

Thank You

Dear Lord,
Thank You!
You answered my prayer!
Everything went all right
  today.
You really helped me, Lord.
I won't feel so frightened
  next time.
Amen.

Dear Lord,
Thank You for my daycare.
I love dressing up,
  playing in the sand box
  and making things.
I like storytime, too.
Thank You for daycare,
  Lord.
Amen.

Dear Lord,
I saw a beautiful rainbow
  this afternoon.
It made me remember the story
  of Noah and the Flood.
Thank You for the rainbow,
  Lord.
Amen.

Dear Lord,
Thank you for television.
My favorite show is...
Please help me not to watch
  too much TV.
Thank You, Lord.
Amen.

Dear God,
Thank You for books to read.
Thank You that we can learn
   things from them and have fun
   reading them.
Amen.

Dear Lord,
Thank You for music.
I like hearing happy songs –
    and singing them, too.
Thank You for making music,
    Lord.
Amen.

Thanks for Food

Dear God,
It's dinner time!
Help us to remember,
  that You give us
  our food each day.
Thank You, Lord.
And please help us with
  our table manners too!
Amen.

Dear Lord,
For our drink,
    for our food,
    for Your gifts that
    are so good,
We thank You, Lord.
Amen.

Heavenly Father,
Thank You for our daily food.
Our tummies are always full!
Please help the poor children
    we see on TV
    who don't get enough to eat
    everyday.
Amen.

45

My Pets

My cat had kittens last
   night, God.
They're so tiny!
Please help them grow up
   big and strong.
Please find them all nice homes
   where they will be loved.
Thank You, Lord.
Oh yes – and I promise I'll
   play gently with them.
Amen.

Dear Lord,
My hamster has died.
Please look after him
  in heaven.
Amen.

People in need

Dear Lord,
Thank You for my new puppy.
He's very naughty.
Please help me to take good
  care of him.
I want him to be happy
  living with us.
Amen.

Dear Lord,
My Mommy works very hard
  to look after me.
She doesn't have much time
  to look after herself.
Please, will You look after her?
I promise to help too.
Amen.

Dear Lord,
I feel sad for all the children
   who don't know You.
They don't know what they're
   missing.
Please help other children
   to learn about You.
Amen.

Dear Father in Heaven,
Please help people in poor
  countries who don't have
  enough to eat.
Please send rain so their
  crops will grow.
Don't let them be forgotten,
  Lord.
Amen.

Sad Times

Dear Lord,
Sometimes my brother and
  sister shout at each other.
I don't like it.
It makes me feel sad inside.
Please help them not to argue.
Then we can all be happy.
I'm glad I can tell you this,
  Lord.
Amen.

Dear Lord,
When I'm sad, please help me
  to be happy again.
Thank You for being with me.
Thank You for understanding
  how I feel.
Amen.

Goodnight!

Dear Lord,
I like it when I lie in bed
  at night and listen to
  the wind and rain.
I feel so cosy and safe.
Thank You for my snuggly
  warm bed.
Please look after all the
  animals and birds outside
  in the cold.
Find them somewhere safe
  and warm.
Thank You, Lord.
Amen.

Dear Lord Jesus,

Please look after me at bedtime.

Sometimes I wake up in the middle of the night and feel scared.

Help me to remember You are always with me and that I don't need to be afraid.

I'm glad You're my friend.

Amen.

I'm Scared!

Dear Lord,
Sometimes I get lonely.
I am too shy to talk
   to anyone.
I feel very left out.
Please help me to fit in
   and make friends.
I know You will always be
   my friend.
Thank You, Lord.
Amen.

Dear Father in Heaven,
I got lost in the shopping
   mall today.
I was very scared.
Mommy got scared too.
I promise never to run off
   on my own again.
I'm sorry.
Thank You for keeping me
   safe, Lord.
I'm glad You were looking
   after me while I was lost.
Amen.

Tomorrow

Dear Lord,
Tomorrow is a very important
  day for me.
You know about it already.
Please look after me tomorrow.
Thank You for listening.
I'm not so worried now.
Amen.

The Children's Friend

Dear Lord Jesus,
You're a friend to all little
   children.
Please be with all unhappy
   children everywhere.
Thank You,
Amen.

Dear God,
Thank You for giving us the
  Bible,
   so we can learn about You.
Amen.

Jesus' prayer

Our Father in heaven,
   help us to honor Your name.
Come and set up Your kingdom soon,
   so that everyone on earth
   will obey You,
   as You are obeyed in heaven.

Give us our food for today.
Forgive us the wrong things
  we have done,
  as we forgive other people.
Keep us from being tempted
  and protect us from evil.
Amen.

MY FIRST BOOK OF PRAYERS
Written by Claire Freedman
Illustrations by Alison Atkins
Copyright © 2008 Lion Hudson plc/
Tim Dowley Associates

Published in 2008 by Candle Books
(a publishing imprint of Lion Hudson plc).

Distributed by Kregel Publications,
PO Box 2607, Grand Rapids, Michigan 49501

Worldwide co-edition produced by
Lion Hudson plc, Wilkinson House,
Jordan Hill Road, Oxford OX2 8DR,
Tel: +44 (0)1865 302750
Fax: +44 (0)1865 302757
Email: coed@lionhudson.com
www.lionhudson.com

ISBN 978 0 8254 7389 0

Printed in Singapore